"Scot Young may not want to hear this, but he isn't a cowboy, not in the movie poster sense anyway. This book, his first, is the history of the man he's become, stronger than his heroes Richard Brautigan and Charles Bukowski, educating young people, publishing countless others without thought given to personal reward, often helping them when they're not in a position to help themselves, opening his heart and sharing a great love of literature, Scot Young is a great poet, but anyone can do that, he's an even greater man, so I take it back, maybe he is a cowboy, but let's be clear, John Wayne would never have the balls to be Scot Young."

-John Dorsey, Author of *The Prettiest Girl at the Dance*

"I find myself reading and rereading the poems in Scot Young's amazing book, *All Around Cowboy*. Scot renders the fundamental "stuff" of life and death in a way that is poignant yet never sentimental. He grew up in a hard place, much as I did. I can identify with his experiences. His lines concerning beer joints, rifles, car wrecks, country music, love and sex, initiation, rock-and-roll, whiskey, drugs, recovery, surviving, and, ultimately, thriving always ring true. This is a book of extraordinary honesty. It's also a remarkable achievement in terms of consistency of tone and style. I highly recommend *All Around Cowboy*."

-W.K. (Kip) Stratton, author of *The Wild Bunch and Betrayal Creek*

"When archeology digs up a book of poetry from this changing planet, it will reveal a bit of "Herodotus Americana" as Scot Young's good cowboy rides into the sunset of the greatest generation and plays the last number on the jukebox. Like the songs, the poems of tragedy and joys, from miniskirts to baseball, grows up and glows up in the middle of the country's golden era of post war years from the 50's to 70's. This all around cowboy knew the greats, from "Butterfly" to "Buk" while metaphorically herding the storm clouds out of the sky. Tragic, rough & rowdy, hip and cool, delicate for the heart and head, his poems, like Robinson, hits the balls and touches all bases, a book I surely dig and so will you, with "Hey good lookin'" on the cover times two. Plus, one can learn his great definition of poetry and discover the worst insult in Western idiom."

-Charles Plymell, author of *Apocalypse Rose, The Last of the Moccasins*

"A beautiful, touching and often insightful journey that hits its mark, Scot Young's *All Around Cowboy* is a country rock rodeo get down. A place suspended in time where Mickey Mantle meets Jack Kerouac on the cosmic baseball diamond with Hendrix on guitar and a lonesome Whippoorwill calling the play by play in the voice of Hank Williams singing my jukebox's got a hole in it. A down to earth collection of first love, brotherly love and true love straight from the heart, these poems are life and death lessons swimming in a swirling beer while sitting in an old school bar called father's office somewhere in the land of sky blue waters."

–S.A. Griffin, Author of *Dreams Gone Mad with Hope*

"A memoir in the form of engaging, finely crafted poems. Vivid, sometimes elegiac, scenes of family life, first and lost loves, poetry and music - all the small and large moments that leave their marks upon the years. The collection has the feel of a jukebox filled with Hank Williams songs, telling you all there is to know about the sweet sorrows of a life lived."

- William Taylor Jr. Author of *Pretty Things to Say*

"There are poems that I've said I wished I'd written…and now there's a book of them. Scot Young's *All Around Cowboy* is an extraordinary, universal poetic journey in what it means to a human being within the world that created us, as we struggle to create it for ourselves. Young's voice, as he weaves his own life's narrative, is one of melancholy and joy over the small moments that we seek out and the moments when we are found; the experiences that make us whole or the ones that blow holes into us. A book of first loves, first losses, late nights in bars with the comfort of words, music and women, *All Around Cowboy* is a tapestry of the human will and spirit."

-John Grochalski, author of the novels, *The Librarian* and *Wine Clerk*

"Scot Young's new book of poetry, *All Around Cowboy*, is filled with firsts: first rock gig, first ballgame, first love crush, first Dodge. He writes of his early dreams back home, Mom and Dad at the center, a child's mind running wild with empathy, considering young mothers from strange towns he's never met, wondering if they too blow bubbles in their dreams. The poems about his barfly father are crushing. Plainly said, brick by brick, the words lay out like a low budget 70's cop caper. You see every move before your eyes, and it's heavy at times. And it's all there, beyond the tavern dust. And Young is never alone. Even when the poet is struggling through a sleepless night, he sniffs at the air and listens quietly for anything recognizable in the house -- the smell of cigarettes, the squeak of linoleum -- and it's in those moments where the poets words are delivered so powerfully."

-Rob Azevedo, *Turning on the Wasp* (Kung Fu Treachery Press, 2020)

"The spirit of the mid-western cowboy lives in the works of Ozark poet Scot Young. Infused with the songs of Hank Williams and with the shadows of Richard Brautigan and Charles Bukowski hanging over like two drunken guardian angels, Young lays bare a life in poetic fashion, telling tales that can't be lived in a post-modern world."

-Daniel W. Wright, author of *Love Letters from the Underground*

ALL AROUND COWBOY

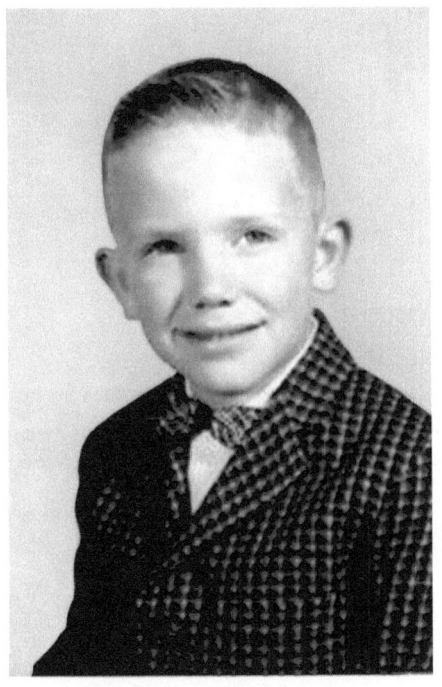

Poems by Scot Young

Kansas City   Spartan Press   Missouri

Spartan Press
Kansas City, Missouri
spartanpresskc.com

Copyright (c) Scot D. Young, 2021
First Edition 1 3 5 7 9 10 8 6 4 2
ISBN: 978-1-952411-53-3
LCCN: 2021932220

Author photo: Scot Young
All rights reserved. No part of this publication may be reproduced or transmitted in any form or by any means, electronic or mechanical, including photocopying, recording or by info retrieval system, without prior written permission from the author.

Acknowledgments:

Lit Circus, Outsider Writers, Rusty Truck, Deuce Coupe, Trailer Park Quarterly, Gasconade Review, Plieadas, Instant Pussy, Black Shark Press, Rye Whiskey Review, Red Fez, Dead Mule, Gutter Eloquence, Opium Poetry, Heroin Long Songs, Covert Poetics, Ragged Lion and *Lit Up.*

TABLE OF CONTENTS

song of myself / 1

the early years / 2

before girls / 3

first day of girls / 4

mothers's bucket / 6

long sad lonesome / 7

decoration day / 9

checking in / 11

long sad lonesome #2 / 13

the greatest generation goes to war / 15

according to the geneva convention / 17

the last lonesome poem ever written / 20

standing outside / 22

the rain doesn't really wash it away / 24

that old time religion / 27

poem for randy / 28

first gig / 32

boys of summer / 33

discography / 35

all my lovin' was the first song / 37

song for maryl / 39

day 1 / 41

between algebra and art / 42

in 1975 before the opioid crisis response act
   of 2018 / 44

march 30, 1973 welcome home / 47

section 60 / 49

veterans park / 51

a study in gender development in 1974 / 52

poem for david / 53

bob drove a mach 1 to the levy / 56

grandma pearl / 57

the jazz of milton morris / 58

ray / 59

tag team champs / 60

brains and eggs after the main event / 61

there is always a girl who listens to my songs
    leaves with some cowboy's hand on her ass
        as i play under these cold blue lights / 63

butterflies on the rocks / 65

next saturday night / 66

open all night / 67

all around cowboy / 69

nobody takes home a stripper / 70

poetry 101 7:45 am / 72

thursday 6th hour / 74

cashed in her mfa / 75

chinatown jazz / 77

being brautigan has not kept up / 78

summer of love minus the vw bus
    and jerry garcia / 79

the ukulele poem / 81

haiku sonnet: brautigan never / 83

i-435 & truman road / 84

valentine love story / 86

front porch spring / 88
sometimes i hold you while you sleep / 89
bottom of the ninth / 90
down a redneck dirt road / 92
haiku sonnet: ozark county / 94
when death comes / 95
singing cowgirl contest / 96
just me and a beat up harmonica / 98
sunday morning / 100
covered in dust waiting for rain / 102
after the game / 104
my vultures / 105
as dillinger waits / 107
feng shui is when she walks out taking the dog
    and the last pack of cigarettes / 108
a haiku love sonnet :
    waiting for the end of yesterday / 109
haiku sonnet: sleeping alone at holiday inn / 110
it's the last verse that nobody knows blues / 111
hank williams a.d. and me / 115
the sun too embarrassed / 116
above the tree line / 119
looking for kerouac / 120
brautigan meets bukowski / 121
bukowski was always right / 123
written in the key of lonely / 124
a beer with bukowski / 125
gone with the wind / 126
one last thing / 128

this book is dedicated to my love rosanna
who once sang on stage at the country playhouse
and when the lights dimmed
threw this cowboy a life preserver

i was drowning in the sea, lost as i could be
when you found me with your boundless love

--john prine

song of myself

in 1960
scot young
watched
hopalong &
roy rogers
from a green
naguhyde sofa
stitched in
cowboys &
bucking broncos
complete with
wagon wheel arms

on saturday mornings
he cocked
his red ryder rifle
before ARs and AKs
before the country
went to hell
in a hate basket
when the good guys
always won

the early years

in 1954
my father bought

mom a new pink &
white dodge

she loved that car
so much she painted

the house to match
the mills brothers sang

*you're nobody till
somebody loves you*

that night
i was conceived

after a couple
cans of heidl brau

and for a brief
moment

all was right
with the world

before girls

we would push our bikes up
the steep hills
then zoom down zig- zagging
like daredevils
wind in our face
drying out the butchwax
made to wear by dad
until we couldn't roll any farther

like a thousand screaming locusts
the maris mantle and mays
rookie cards clothes-pinned
to our spokes turning
our schwinns into
wannabe triumphs

old man smith would yell
as we flew by
you little dumb asses
was all we could make out
for that summer we were
the wild ones spitting
gnats from our teeth

first day of girls

in seventh grade
first hour i saw
carmela occhipinti
big italian smile
ta-tas to match
orange mini dress
off-white polka dots
are there bombshells
at 13
never saw this
in elementary
those chocolate eyes
cut right to the center
of a 7th grade
boy's heart
nothing else mattered
before or after

that polka dot image
was burned into this
kid's brain
testosterone &
awkwardness
raced to every corner
of my body
as i stumbled
into the chair beside her

slouched in jeans
white t-shirt
checked her out
through the corner
of my eye
checking me out
through the corner
of hers

today i learned
through some reunion site
she had died
breast cancer
of all damn things
and it made me sad
i hoped her life
was good
as i saw her
in that mini dress
and remembered
how many times
i dropped my pencil

mothers's bucket

we often dream the dreams
we'll forget in the morning
but each night
you hover above us
angel wings touching
the tip of the moon
holding your bucket of blue stars
dropping each one gently

they protect us
you make sure of that
and somewhere in the city
a young mother blows bubbles
with their child for the first time

i wonder if you were dropping
blue stars there too

long sad lonesome

found these three poems
written about dad
how she missed him
loved him
hurt for him
how she wanted to call
him when she felt
that long sad lonesome

i never knew
she wrote poems
never said how she felt
after she left him
but these poems cried
& moaned the long
sad lonesome
when she died
he sat all day
over a beer
felt her go again

hank williams sang
all those sad songs
those lonesome songs
enough beer and hurt
to make him go
home early

one year later
patsy's faded love
played background
at his funeral
it was his poem
his manifesto of
i miss you darling…
his way of saying
goodbye to the long
sad lonesome
his way of saying
just how much

decoration day

it is on this day
and every other
i remember
you did not serve
on any front
but fought
the life war
battling vices
and dad

struggling
to either
join him
or
leave him
you chose both
neither worked

fighting
for a shred of
normality
you thought
others had
and you deserved
you lost

i send this kiss

on angel wings
maybe too late
to comfort
your soul
but
it is on this day
and every other
i remember

checking in

it is usually when
i come home
walk through the door
of birthdays and
christmas mornings
or late at night
when for no reason
i wake shaken
heart beating too fast
to catch the brief
smell of cigarettes
partially covered by
the scent of your
red door perfume

the sound of wind
that rattles louvers
in the attic
that one spot
that squeaks
by the fridge
when the cat
walks across
worn linoleum
it is when
the furnace kicks on
i hear you call

feel the patchwork
warmth that tucks me in
one more time
trying to make sense of it
i doze back off
content knowing
you were just
checking in

long sad lonesome #2

my mother died in 93
after too many years
of tareytons and
viceroys
my father a year later
they found him in his shower
after a couple days

he hit his head
the water still running
i never was told if he was drunk
if it was his heart or he just slipped
the facts didn't matter
it was a slow motion suicide
that took 73 years
one can at a time

they divorced in 1975
went their separate ways
but their hearts never did
they never talked about it
after that
but you saw that light
in their eyes
if only for a second
if you mentioned the other

faded love by patsy cline
i miss you darlin
more and more everyday
played at his funeral

it was his song
B3 on the last lonely
jukebox in the hangout bar
just off raytown road

the greatest generation goes to war

tom brokaw said you were from the
greatest generation but you went 4F
instead of being inducted with your brothers
instead of storming the beach at normandy
the army said not acceptable for military service
you were not good enough
to be the first to die when they dropped the ramp

the greatest generation didn't talk about the war
and your war stories were never discussed
you disappeared for weeks on induction day
never dropped the ramp to hit the beach
or ever stopped to let others aboard
but spent the next 50 years going 4F
drowning in the land of sky blue waters
most days after work wrapping
yourself around a can or bottle
trying to forget or was it
to remember

every other saturday we would get a haircut
at joe's & stop in at the hangout bar for a couple
you sat at the table when you had me go along
wasn't right for a kid to sit at the bar you'd say
at age seven i asked you once
daddy what do you do in the war
you swirled your beer in the glass

those blue eyes narrowed
looking right through me
drank it down
ordered another
asked if i wanted another coke
and don't tell your mother
we were here

they say you never ask
the greatest generation about the war
the ones that made it back will take
the stories to their grave
the ones that never made it
will do the same
every single day

according to the geneva convention

when i was seven i
would go with you
and uncle ben to the lake
we would sit in barker's
bar up the steep hill
next to the stone gas station
with one pump
you guys would cuss
drink foam out of frosty mugs
i would spin around on the stool
until you fed me nickels
to play endless games of shuffle board
and the bowling game
with collapsible plastic pens

sometimes i would chase
the minnows around
the tank out front of barker's
on the lake
one time you let me
drive the speed boat
with the faded red cadillac fins
to another bar on the lake
about two beers away

i remember a wild goat
curved back horns
standing on the narrow ledge
above the main channel
watching us bounce through the waves
like a runaway torpedo
water splashing against my face

isn't it funny what we remember
you would have me play B19 on the jukebox
5 cents to get me out of earshot
while you guys patted
the waitress on her backside

it was when
you guys slept late
i mostly fished for perch
off the dock
it was my game
when they started to nibble
pull up the bait
so they wouldn't be caught
and you wouldn't have
to cut off their heads
i would come up the 27 stairs
empty stringer about the time
you guys got up

nope
not biting today
i'd say

at home
mom would ask
what we did
i told her we had a blast
only gave her my
name
rank
and
serial
number

the last lonesome poem ever written

i was about six
when my dad said
this is hank
opened a can from the land
of sky blue
and sang
i'm so lonesome i could cry

he sang all the sad songs
the lonesome songs
without a woman cause
she done me wrong songs
he passed down in that garage
on those saturday mornings
the lonesome gene
as i listened wide eyed
wanting *she loves you yeah yeah*
but got
there's a tear in my beer
i knew nothing of dna

it developed slow but
stayed nurtured
hung on like a slide guitar
hung on like the last
minor chord ringing
before the fade out

like being broke
at last call

it is the lonely yodel
of being loved
by a good woman
and still hearing him say
on some lonesome
saturday morning
this is hank

standing outside

it was just now i realized
what drew you
to the hangout bar
it was your grown up
clubhouse
just like the fort where
little boys took comfort
and looked out on the world
through a camouflaged
peep hole
it was a secret this place
where we kept
our treasures buried
under a rock
cigarettes wrapped
in cellophane
it was this fort
that held you on too
many christmas eves
on birthdays and friday nights
on almost every time
you were supposed to be

i stopped in
the first time
in many years
someone else sat

on your stool
i watched from a corner
table as he swirled
his last bit of beer
in a short glass
threw it down
head back
eyes closed
then nodding
through his camouflage
at the bartender
rearranged his keys
and stacked
jukebox quarters
beside a holiday coaster

the rain doesn't really wash it away

after 50 years
the details get blurry
like the rainy night
a block from harvey's
tavern where you lay
bleeding
lifeless
on that rain soaked
highway
i remember i was invited
to the movies that night
my mother said no

i pass your grave
when we travel
go out of the way
to pass by
sometimes we stop
find your marker
until taking a deep breath
doesn't really help

i am reminded of the day
our junior high closed
one hour parade

of buses down
50 highway
crying through your service
sitting shoulder to shoulder
many outside never got in
lined around downtown
warrensburg
except to file by your casket
and picture
blonde bangs beatle haircut
ever smiling face
i remember our teachers
were quiet that day
taking up the back rows
adult silent crying

after 50 years the details
get blurry
like when the windshield wipers
don't remove all
the water
and the rain really doesn't
 wash it all away
it is the same as
not understanding
about losing a friend
at 13

nobody talked
on the way home
white faced
we stared
out the bus windows
not knowing we
would never
be the same

that old time religion

for mitzi jo

near sundown
you taught me
by example how to
french kiss
near the back
of the church bus
    blanket across our laps
waiting for it to get
a little bit darker

poem for randy

someone said
way before
we were born
that time heals
all wounds
well
i remember
we wore ties
back then for school pictures
our moms made us
they did the best
they could
teaching us to walk
the line when we
didn't necessarily
 want to
i remember when you asked
me to go to the movies &
and my mom said no
she never met your parents...

moms said that back then
it was a mom rule
then at 13 and 14
 we learned

what shock was
that it was ok to cry
though most of us tried to
hold it back at your funeral
some for 50 plus years

now
when a see a young boy
getting his school picture taken
wearing a tie
i think of you
when i hear a beatles song
i think of you
when i pass thru warrensburg
i stop and we talk
i guess it gets easier
the older i get

when i see a young kid
with straight blonde bangs
i think of you

i see you at 14 smiling
sharing a basket of fries
on some saturday
 at blue ridge bowl
we sang steppenwolf
playing the first air guitar in the world

we thought we were born
to be wild
grabbing whb's
top 40 list at jenkin's music
 and eating cream
filled long johns
from next door
when i think of you
 i see gail and you holding hands
in the hallway
and how you two kids
fit perfectly together
slow dancing at
the sock hop

 i remember playing
the back nine at
stayton meadows and
you showed me to how
to grip the club
when i think of you
it is mainly about
the holes
you left
about the holes you left
in a few hundred
hearts

and as for
 time healing

well
 i found out
later
it only
slows
the
bleeding

first gig

we were a teenage cover band
played *louie louie*
wipeout & *house of the risin sun*
from the back of a hay wagon
right behind the original
jc penney
hamilton missouri
my mama's town
my family tree
sitting around squinting
into the setting sun

great uncle whit
just starched overalls
pointing one shaky finger
at me singing
said oh hell
them's city boys
turned and
spit brown juice
in an empty cup
ten feet away

boys of summer

in 1965
dad took me to my first
baseball game
kansas city a's
municipal stadium on brooklyn
down by 18th & vine
saw my first black kid up close
parked our impala in his yard
next to the porch
for a buck

his whole family sat spread out
across the porch
the black man
collecting dollar bills
smiled a lot and shook his
head up and down
the boy and i stared
at each other
maybe waiting for the other
to blink

the a's normally lost
and that afternoon
campy campaneris played
every position
as a publicity stunt

dad made me a magaphone
out of paper beer cups
to cheer the kelley green and gold
after the game i carried
my pennant back to the car
peanuts stuffed in my pockets
nobody was on the porch
& the a's of course lost
that summer i wanted
to be called campy
playing our sandlot ball
on vacant lots
a white cuban growing up in the burbs
in 1965 we all wanted something
we couldn't have

discography

after school
in the mid 60s
at the malt shop
jukebox   i listened
to sam the sham's
little red riding hood
and the song
leader of the pack
we were am radio rebels
eating cheeseburgers
and cherry phosphates

but at night we listened to
clyde clifford's
beaker street
from little rock
50,000 watts of
album cuts & acid rock
slipped slowly like
a mickey finn
into our midwest
cookies & milk

in the garage
we smoked viceroys taken
from mom's purse
learned how to blow

smoke rings to the pre pop
sound of
zappa & zeppelin
began tuning guitars
 to the chords of
eric burden &
steppenwolf
girlfriends getting
in the groove
in the backseat
of a 63 chevy

all my lovin was the first song

in 64 i was nine
all the boys loved mary beth
not for what she had done
but we had seen sixth graders
walk down the hall
holding hands
and we were looking ahead

one sunday night
ed sullivan stepped aside
and said *the beatles*
the young girls cried
and every boy in america
was set free
grew bangs
bought black suede beatle boots
and a cheap silvertone guitar

close your eyes and i'll kiss you
was a line that worked
at the first make out party
taking turns in the closet
before the beatles discovered
the marhareshi and yoko
when ringo still wore a ring
on every finger

not sure what happened
to mary beth
the boots
the single pickup guitar
playing simple three chord
love songs
sometimes we break or lose
our past
sometimes mom would sell
it at a garage sales.

song for maryl

we broke up in 69
my band played
your junior high dance
and i sang you a song
 i just wrote
 about our teen love
and broken hearts
brought you to tears
which was probably
 my intent

we moved on as kids do
never spoke again
at 23 you wrote
 your own song
about broken hearts
with carbon monoxide
in a closed up garage
full tank of gas
slow idle

i never
wrote another song
for no other reason
than just because
i don't remember
the lyrics now but

50 years later
 i can still
see your eyes
every time
you smiled
 i will sing that
song
i know
all the words

day 1

1972
teenage sex
under a cheesy moon
eight track plays
croce low volume
time in a bottle
sets the mood
top down gives
us more room
you borrowed
your sister's
28 days of kama sutra
we had 20 minutes
before the porch light
came on
i prayed for 27 more
days just like
this one

between algebra and art

i've only seen one apple machine
in my life
it dispensed cold red delicious apples
between classes for a dime
it had a glass front so you could
see the beads of condensation
& when the light was just right
it doubled as a mirror
it was right after paul announced the break up
& the world hated yoko
& apollo 13 barely made it back
& at the isle of wight
600,000 watched hendrix for probably the last time
& the evening news declared women
were still burning their bras
myth or not
the times had changed

between algebra and art
i fell in love
everyday i would
watch debbie
at that machine
waiting
for the apple to drop
slow motion

if you were older
she'd say

little white halter top
stretched
over olive skin
cher straight dark hair
clearly a believer of the liberation
& that single daily ritual
when the light and the shadows
were just right
the most important
event in the world

and see if you google
significant events of 1970
you'll find
1. u.s. invades cambodia
2. chicago 7 found guilty
3, first earth day celebration
4. four dead in ohio
5. debbie buys an apple
   makes young boy smile
   between algebra and art

in 1975 before the opioid crisis response act
of 2018

greg
got
addicted
to
methadone
after
he
lied
about
being
hooked
on
heroin

the
clinic
gave
it
away
daily

on
fridays
you
got
a

weekend
supply
he'd
shoot
it
up
right
there
sitting
in
his
mom's
98
nodding
off
like
death
dragging
a
crippled
foot

outside
an
old
woman
pulled
a
grocery
cart

up
the
paseo
like
he
wasn't
even
there

march 30, 1973 welcome home

i remember
nobody wanted to go
but you did
instead of going to canada
or taking a college deferment
or joining the national guard
your daddy drove a truck
had nobody to pull strings

i remember that you enlisted
before graduation
shipped off without a party
or a big damn hullabaloo
went off to vist ho chi minh
with a m16 & a ka bar strapped
to your side

i remember you still had pimples
on your face and favored aqua velva
and double bubble when you left
you returned
without a party
a thank you
or go to hell
well maybe you did get that

i remember you came back silent
carrying other scars
the ones hidden deep inside
like family secrets
most cutting too deep to ever heal
today i learned that congress declared
30 march welcome home
vietnam veterans day
38 damn years too late
so here's your party mac
sorry you didn't live
to see it but the guilt
is now washed clean
and ain't that something

section 60

the wind blows
most days in
section 60
as children &
mothers &
fathers &
wives &
you
leave
small stones
on white marble
so others will know
between the silence
you rub the name
with blue crayola
for the fridge
at home
on the hour
the sobs muffled
by iron bells
you listen
like something will
change
like the wind will
blow it all away

like tears of angels
on white marble
just might
make a difference

veterans park

he was drafted
a hot prospect
by the giants in 67
infantryman
by the army in 68
somewhere north
of the mekong delta
pitching for charlie company
mai lai
with the bases loaded
he blew out his mind

today
no dugouts or bullpens
in this ward of word slobber
he stands bent
staring home
through eastwood eyes
waiting for a sign
dust dancing
in the sunlight
like confetti
from the world series

a study in gender development in 1974

you were walking to a downtown lunch
i was one of the construction workers
hanging out the 8th floor window
grabbing my crotch
wolf whistle   yelling
hey ba-by

you stopped
whirled around &
gave us a combination of
shove it up your ass and the finger
in one fluid motion
we all laughed
slapped each other on the arm
looked down the street for the next

but that was before research told us
the frontal lobe in males developed
slower than females
before i became a father
of three daughters
(who sometimes like to have
lunch downtown when)
i was just an asshole

poem for david

i remember when
marijuana was $15 oz
i was neal cassady
on that magic bus
zig-zagging
across the south
nonstop to jamaica
teenagers caught
free in america

i remember
you threw up
in that arkansas midnight
taking ludes w/o water
falling out of the car
flat on that blue highway
you would do anything
to keep from driving
you laughed
looking like a
half assed
snow angel
laid out
on that delta asphalt

28 years
since i have

seen you
not that we haven't
thought or spoke
your name
i tried to picture
you in a nursing home
couldn't imagine
blocked it out

we got a letter
saying you died
i was angry
not that you were gone
but for other reasons
maybe for the way you lived
or didn't
or could have
maybe for the way
they walked over you
your brains on that porch
that black damned night
as the ambulance
pulled away
maybe because you
never found the
easy way to make
a buck
your get rich quick
schemes always
fell apart

but you would quickly
come up with another

i don't normally do funerals
but
would have done yours
would have wrote
a long poem
celebrating your life
cried reading it   would have read
something from
kerouac's scroll
like fabulous yellow roman candles
exploding
like spiders across the stars

and slipped something
under your hand for
your trip
i would have looked
deep into your face
behind that little
shit eating grin
you always wore
seen our past
like a childhood
flipbook
and said good-bye

bob drove a mach 1 to the levy

bob didn't know
facebook or believe
in poets
 but thought in terms
of clevelands and windsors
of fastback mustangs
of busted knuckles &
greasy coveralls
he never got thoughts
and prayers posted
online but before
he died
wild bill brought
him a carton of
lucky strikes
that lasted him
to the finish line

grandma pearl

standing outside the old
jc penneys
hamilton missouri
barn wood face
faded print dress
over a bent frame
knee hose rolled
watches tourists
tying down
genuine amish buggy wheels

now they'll go stick 'em
in the ground
she tells me
some days it's better than
a picture show

the jazz of milton morris

we held our union
meetings upstairs
but downstairs
at the tap room
milton morris sold
kansas city
jazz & juice
friend of basie
parker and young

and during prohibition
since both were illegal
he sold whiskey and reefer
25 cents
for medicinal purposes
only

but it was the jazz
that hooked you
the blue haze
& cool saxophone
drifting down main
like a lonely lady
in a red dress
lingering
selecting
a slow song
on the last
jukebox
ever made

ray

got outta prison in 82
pulled up to the job site in a caddy
trunk full of sansabelts
banlons and a dozen leather jackets
big bob said
hell ray we don't wear that shit
got any flannel shirts & jeans

ray
narrowed his eyes
like eastwood in hang 'em high
remembering the last thing
his daddy said right before
he hit the ground

best part of you ran down
your momma's leg

tag team champs

dirty dick murdoch
and i shared the mic
on mama tried
with a whiskey twang
of too much jack
and a left over
choke hold
after a championship
match
ready to body slam
the world

we took the stage
with the cadillac cowboys
in midtown
cowtown
and became merle
and lefty
two of the
toughest sonsabitches
ever to sing
off key

brains and eggs after the main event

we
left
jerry's
after
the
bar
closed
in
bulldog's
eldorado
headed
to nichol's
lunch
when
murdoch
pulled
a .357
spun
the
cylinder
& shot
a hole
through
the
backseat
floorboard
at 39th
& main

when
my
ears
quit
ringing
we
were
halfway
through
our
brains
and eggs

there is always a girl who listens to my songs
leaves with some cowboy's hand on her ass
as i play under these cold blue lights

the silver buckle rests
in the groove worn
on the back of this
pawn shop guitar
one pant leg half
in my boot
the other out
cigarettes dance
close to the tuners
as smoke rises
to the same three chords

too many fights
in this stetson
pulled down
scarred by saturday nights
shaped with spilled beer

i always sing this willie song
about rain and blue eyes
and watch ours
never meet

when i look up
your empty glass

on the bar
says you're gone and
nobody in this dive
gives two shits
about sad songs

butterflies on the rocks

bends over
shows the red lace

stretched against
silk skin

she slowly adds ice
to a new drink

watching the clock
tick saturday night

seconds of lonely
i fold dollar

bills into
origami butterflies

next saturday night

we make eye contact through cigarette smoke
sometime between mamma tried & i walk the line
something about short shorts and your ride a cowboy
t shirt and boots that make you stand out
it will take a while   few more drinks
maybe a few shots but you will ask me
to dance and at last call we will dance down the sidewalk
end up at your place

without a bunch of small talk
another shot of tequila we will have some hot shooting
out the lights sex and pass out
i will wake up in the morning
head pounding
see the sheet twisted around your long leg
briefly study the curve in your back
find my pants and before i need to recall your name
i leave boots in hand
ride the high lonesome back home
wonder if this is all there is

open all night

i stumble out of last night
into sunday morning
beating the church
crowd to denny's
i keep a sweat stained
poem folded inside
my hat under the band

i pull it out sometimes
between night and morning
between a boilermaker
and a grand slam
when i leave alone
and all the sadness
poured in a glass
at closing time
follows me down
the sidewalk kicking
me in the ass

tonight i unfold it
unable to make out
the words
under the sepia glow
of old downtown
i open my hand
let the wind

an urban blender
of lonesome
mix the pieces
with old cigarettes
and blowing paper

waiting to cross
the street
i wonder
how many times
something is lost
on sunday mornings
just like this one

all around cowboy

after the rodeo
at cottonwood falls
we drank beer
out of my stetson
danced on brick streets
to bob wills
the texas swing
leaving my hat on
after too many longnecks
we made love
beside my old truck
like i was the last
cowboy on earth

nobody takes home a stripper

we were building
a power plant in
st marys kansas in
1978
tasha
just in from whicita
had dolly platinum hair
 and danced
with a boa constrictor
at charlie hall's
golden horseshoe
i can't tell you why
i thought taking her home
to meet my mother
was a good idea
it wasn't
mom grilled her on
quilting
canning
sewing
the conversation
flat lined
after tasha told her
about her job
and the snake

our third night together
tasha put carrots
in the orange jello

just to see she said
it was a test she said

she packed up in 43 minutes
and headed back to topeka
the counterfeit jello
jiggled as the door slammed

in the early 60s
my elementary teachers
didn't pull any punches
not everybody got
a blue ribbon
grade cards had checklists
mine said
does not behave well
in the cafeteria

does not test well

poetry 101 7:45 am

i never sat with brautigan
in a north beach bar
or hid out with bukowski
in the city of angels
but if i had
i may have learned early
what the pages
don't reveal

instead
i taught a poetry class
to your abused broken
 and neglected children
and started to give
them metaphors
similes & personification
but they knew figurative language
well enough and tried to wear
the face of normal
wanting to be like other kids
tried to hide the scars
with just inked tattoos and too
much massacre

they read their poems
of incest
of rape

of beatings
of parents in prison
of foster homes
of being hooked on meth made
down a dead end country road
of how life is not supposed
to be at age 15

they learned that giving
human characteristics
to inanimate objects
sometimes lessened the pain
but i changed my lesson
plan when one of them said
hey teach
what is good poetry

i suppose it is keeping
your wounds close
to the surface so they can heal
quicker

is that it

on most days
it is

thursday 6th hour

i sat cross legged
on the hallway floor
she sat huddled
against locker 17
said when she cuts
and the blood
starts to flow
it relieves the
pain
allows her to make another day
allows her
to finally
feel something

she tucks her head
between her knees
like practicing
for a tornado drill
taps her finger
on her jeans

cashed in her mfa

she wears plaid skirts
knee socks on saturday nights
drinks too much &
lets bald men spank her
for money &
tell her she's been a bad girl
but there's enough freaks
to pay the bills
put her kid through college
so she quit writing
poetry
a long time ago

on sundays she wears
fishnets to church
sits on the front pew
gives the preacher
a little hell fire
of his own
crosses & slowly uncrosses
her legs enough
that he yells
during the children's service

hallelujah
give me an amen

stays behind the pulpit
until way after
the sermon was over

chinatown jazz

sax man blows
slow note jazz
corner of kearny
& california
bubbles up like
a slo-gin fizz
in a hip pocket
flask
sun glasses
lowered
case open
catches loose change
from tourists
walking too fast
to feel
the jazzman's
wail
that wraps the walls
of old st mary's

being brautigan has not kept up
with inflation

at folsom
and embarradero
they cast the poem
30 cents
two transfers
into the sidewalk
today i realized
that riding
this world
alone will cost
you two dollars
not exactly
an economic indicator
but still a bargain
on lonesome

summer of love minus the vw bus and jerry garcia
haight 2009

brown skinned girl
in cha cha cha
gently licked
jerk sauce
from her fingers
ck sunglasses replace
leather headbands
and who wears
a flower
in her hair
each finger
disappeared
between
wet lips
a freeze frame
one by one
softly touching
the tongue that
never tasted
baez when she
sang virgil kane
or played guitar
on the corner
of haight & ashbury
on the first day
of the rest of our lives

big black
sephora eyes
danced madly
to a marley song
not wanting to
waste single drop

the ukulele poem
for abby

yoko said poetry should ring
of the soul or sing of the soul
(i can never remember)
but paul wanted to play
the ukulele not piano
on the last album
& lennon sang
*whisper words of wisdom
let it be a*nd it was never the same
after that

and tiny tim only marched
through the tulips
never tip toed
& when he needed
a valium it was not
miss vickie that kept
him balanced
she curled his hair
the ukulele gave
him peace

my daughter bought a ukulele
in haight the other day
carried it be her side
like machine gun kelly

past this week's
self imposed
street kids who eyed
her up and down
didn't buy it for don ho
or tip toe flower tunes
but a baritone uke
built to beat the blues
with every three chord
hank williams song
cause nobody asks for spare
change or breaks the heart
of a woman singing
move it on over

haiku sonnet: brautigan never

brautigan never
wrote a haiku love sonnet
and nailed it to a

street lamp in downtown
san francisco so you would
walk by and see it

on a moon beam night
just like this one   a poem
a bay breeze moving

it just enough so
you will notice before turn
ing on market but

on this night it will be raining
in love just like he said

i-435 & truman road

there are three homeless guys
living under the bridge
on truman road
you can see their
damp blankets
cardboard
water bottles lined up
tucked under the steel
each have a section for sleep
share the sound of a semi
and sirens on their ceiling
they spend the day
sitting
on plastic buckets
holding signs
homeless
hungry
waiting for a window
to roll down
you know the guys
the bucket
the sign
the cold stares
like a dull sun
shining off a winter lake
like waiting
for the ice to freeze
enough for christmas skates

you see them
everyday
through tinted glass
then turn away
like that child
afraid if the ice breaks
you will have to ask
for help

valentine love story

the guy who fixed
my furnace today told
me how he lost his wife
nine years ago at age 40
left him 3 young children
how it took seven damn years for
cancer to finally win the war

about how they met at age 12
in small town usa
how they climbed trees
built forts
stretched out on the ground
watching clouds
grew up together in love
holding hands
about how she was
his best friend
still is

that her last words that day
were hold me
and he did
still does

i asked him if he ever
remarried

he looked at me
said naw how could i
ever find someone like her
and went back fixing
my furnace

sometimes i wish
i could take
words back

front porch spring
a haiku dirt road sonnet

brown hills sprinkled with
white blooms of serviceberry
waiting for dogwoods

crappie huddled up
on old christmas trees weighted
for this shallow cove

overnight pop of
green finally hides the light
of next hill neighbor

fawns freeze in driveway
scattered sweet william backdrop
of almost redbuds

whippoorwills will return as
if they never left

sometimes i hold you while you sleep

somewhere
between the road signs
hi & dri boat storage
and
have you talked to the lord today

i looked over
watched you sleep
chest
gently lifts
caught in window light
prisms
angels pirouette
on rainbows

as we passed
through egypt grove
dylan sang
blowin in the wind
i said a quiet prayer

bottom of the ninth

--for bob church

we grew up playing until dark
be home before
the street lights came on
mowing vacant lots
marking the bases
with scraps of wood
or cardboard
sandlot baseball
a past time passion
we were outside kids
wanting to be mantle
knocking it out
of the park or
drysdale striking out
the side in the last game
of the world series

we grew up
butch wax flat tops
gap tooth smiles
blue jeans rolled up
and dirty knees
catching crawdads
from the creek
with bacon and string

sometimes making
both love and war
we went looking
for that american dream
doing our own thing
our own way
finding nothing ever
remains the same
and there is no
yellow brick road

we shed some blood
along the way and
in that blood found
the real dream
was not a picket fence
2.5 children
a cadillac in every pot
but the love of a
good woman
arms holding us tight
waiting for us
one day
to wake up

down a redneck dirt road

where the dirt
meets the blacktop
donna has a camo tarp
stretched over her life
of bags
& boxes &
all she could carry

this is not common
in ozark county
nobody goes homeless
on a redneck dirt road
but donna did at 64 years
and 80 pounds
i took her bottled water
asked her what happened
she cried and told me
the stories of every
thing she had lost
in the last 30 years
those that done
her wrong but
she said she believed
in angels
and saints
and god
had a plan

i asked if she could call anyone
i'm out of minutes
she said
bobby is supposed to pick me up

you can use mine if you like
she looked away
an suv drove
by and honked
if you love jesus
she yelled

donna didn't pan
handle didn't have
a sign with
anything will help
she just sat in a camp chair
on a redneck dirt road
with worn out dreams
infected blisters
on her ankles
paperback in her lap
waiting for angels
waiting for saints
waiting for bobby
and tonight
it is going to rain

haiku sonnet: ozark county

hands held on weathered
glades set with yellow primrose
side step cactus that

stair steps down through oak
scattered woods hidden from noon
day tourists lost and

dodging dirt road ruts
their path leads to our hidden
waterfall off that

ridge spilling into
a shaded pool reflecting
soft blooms of dogwoods

in filtered light we
scratch our names on mossy rocks

when death comes

we buried ashton today
he was 19 half blind
and deaf
i dug a hole next
to the mother mary statue
in the secret garden
my wife held
him for hours
stroked his head
talked to him in low tones
and sang funny little
cat songs that only cats
can understand
she lined the hole
with lemon balm and lavender
wrapped him in a towel

i hope i die before her
so she is there
to sing me songs
talk in low tones
but that would mean
she would be alone
it is never easy
planning your own
death

singing cowgirl contest

for rosanna

you
played
piano
sang
some
patsy
on
that
cowboy
saturday
night
kentucky
whiskey
with a
colt
tucked
inside
my
vest
i
played
my
last
hand &
after
the

lights
went
out
we
sang
our
own
song
just
trying
to
get
the words
right

just me and a beat up harmonica

no this aint hank williams
not even luke the drifter
singing those preachy songs
with the lonesome wail
of a steel guitar

but just me with four notes
on a beat up harmonica
that makes even
you are my sunshine
sound like the blues
and we learn fast that
slide guitars never play
no love songs

and nobody slow dances
like that anymore
i think the whole beat changed
when we quit using words
like sweetheart
and darlin

so it's just me caught
in this world of sad songs
where even silent night holy night
sounds like a 12 bar riff

i don't believe the blues
was born in mississippi
but here in this valley
under a too bright moon
collar turned up against the cold with
two thousand jewels in the sky

it is almost a kodak moment
but no angels will hover above me
and no one will sing hallelujah

alone tonight
i will play the only song i know
carried by the wind
echoed
by the whippoorwills
as i sing

come sit by my side
if you love me

i will hold the last note
for as long
as i can

sunday morning

buster
redbone hound
sleeps soundly
on the front porch
stretched out taking
in the morning sun
dreaming of the next hunt
you are in the house
frying bacon
making scratch biscuits
maple flavor drifts through
the open window
you sing streisand
it sounds good
paired against
these ozark hills
almost spiritual
bringing culture
to this holler
blue car stops
in the driveway
jehovah's witness
steps out
begins the conversation
ol buster raises up
barks slightly
looks him straight

in the eye
and begins
licking his balls
like any good
coon dog
would do
on a perfect
sunday morning

covered in dust waiting for rain

this old truck tucked
just into the woods
off a dirt road
cedar growing
through its skeleton
used to haul
people
wood
field dressed deer
during season or not
sometimes moonshine
up and down these
ozark roads paved
in mud and chert

old man penley
left it here one day
got pissed off
cause it wouldn't
pull the hill
loaded full of wood
backed off in the trees
and left it
came back a half
dozen times
stripped it clean
nothing left now

but a speedometer
one chrome bumper
just sits
permanently parked
sometimes a summer
house for roadrunners
but always rusting
a shell of the 50s
neighbors pass by
occasionally
nod toward the truck
and say
that penley
he was a crazy
sumbitch

after the game

thanksgiving dinner is over
at the local vfw
packed with old vets smoking
non filters &
swisher sweets
swirling lonesome ice
in hi ball glasses

the lions game is over
as well as the yelling
& cussing
john prine plays
on the juke box
the speed of the sound of loneliness

sam stone came home
kicked off the quiet

big jim said he is thankful
for the other guys
it is early
and the remembering
has just begun

my vultures
for fn wright

i saw two turkey buzzards
roosting
outside my door
holding vigil
in the treetops
like the undertaker
in high plains drifter

watching
as i walked
to the barn to feed
and back
to the front porch

they usually circle
these rusty truck hills
and hollers looking
for the dead

but today they sit
motionless
waiting
not riding the currents
frozen to the limb
daring me to blink

as i loaded my rifle
closed one eye
studied them through
the crosshairs
they flew away

today they win this one
and so do i

as dillinger waits
for todd moore

an outlaw
shot the last
colt forty
five
ricocheting
through the
universe
like tequila
shot glasses
slammed on a
sawdust floor
and tonight
lola
will dance
for no one

feng shui is when she walks out taking the dog
and the last pack of cigarettes

nine times out of 10
when she says she means it, she
really does mean it.

a haiku love sonnet :
waiting for the end of yesterday

sometimes we travel
deep into this naked night
and see yesterday

eager to reconstruct
bits of a fragmented dream
with lost dialogue

wait for fading light
to kiss the soft of angel
wings warmed by the day

not an easy job
turning the orange sky dark
not an easy job

rearranging the planets
hanging a blue moon

haiku sonnet: sleeping alone at holiday inn

couple next room too
much wine too much viagra
64 minutes

not wanting to be
outdone i moaned crescendo
take it all—baby

oh yeah that's it — who's
your big daddy — c'mon girl…
standing on the bed

i increased the speed
headboard against the shared wall
as leno finished

his monologue i screamed yes!
65 minutes`

it's the last verse that nobody knows blues

from California
this land is singing
to the new York island
the blues
12 bar field hollers
ring from slave shacks
blues

the smoke rises
in mississippi jukejoints
foot stomp
on the down beat
bend the e string
on pawn shop guitars
of bo diddley boxes
shoeboxmade on a worn
slick shotgun porch
blues

the heat rises
cigarettes burn in neck strings
old blues is played
eyes closed with
black cat bones
on the edge of a swamp
with too many gators
in the no moon night

of the backdoor man
sneaking out
blues

part of a cc rider doin'
a free ride
it is king of the delta
blues man teaching us
how to play slide
on a flat top
blues

the fog rises
we hitch with woody
see san francisco wail
the blues
singing the taptaptap needle
on homeless sidewalks
singing the somebody's
little girl turned walking
the midnight sidewalk
wanna date   got some shit
blues

the sound rises
through the f holes
we walk the line
of ramshackle housing
heat turned off
of absent fathers

moved out
moved on
of halfway houses
of safe houses
of crack houses
of a factory set up
to fail the huddled masses
w/o a house
blues

the flag raised
to the screaming
silent blues
of walter reed teaching
heroes how to walk
on one leg
it is the blues riff
of *yearning to breathe free*
it is grade school children
learning
god shed his grace on thee
for the first time
blues

it is the foot stomp
on the down beat
the taptaptap
slap on the cracked
guitar blues
when we are

still humming the tune
eyes closed
but have forgotten
the words

hank williams a.d.
and me

nobody since
has had the corner
on lonely
on country blues
so lonesome that everything
written a.d. is plagiarized
robbed in broad daylight

i know
my bucket's got a hole in it
but not large enough to let the
lonesome slide through
but big enough
to let the light leak in

part of that line
belongs to hank
i guess the lonesome
part is mine
well maybe i stole that too

and in the missouri dark
jesse james rode alone

the sun too embarrassed

for mike

i heard when johnny cash died
that dylan said *he was*
the north star
that you could guide your
ship by

i remember you shifting
thru the gears of
your midnight green
65 chevelle
mickey thompson mags
on the way to mugs up
to see yr best girl

and how you always
did the right thing
playing it safe
never taking risks
never going head on
into that goodnight

i remember how
 multiple wives
& roommates each
altered your dna
just enough

before
cleaning you out
how each one chipped
away at you
until
there was only dust

i can tell you
it was good weather
for a funeral
the sun
 too embarrassed
to show its face

but it is
never a good day
except for those
that cashed in
and stood
graveside
blank faced
with hands in their pockets

and you know
that girl from mugs up
was the only one to speak
when asked for comments
she broke the quiet awkwardness
said you had the best smile
and stopped left it at that

but i knew there was more
that wasn't said

hiding behind sunglasses
and fighting tears
 i remembered the way
you laughed the most

walking to the car
when everyone
promised to keep
in touch
i repeated
in my head
hoping you could hear

growing up
you
were my
johnny cash

above the tree line

lew
welch wrote
his last poem
at snyder's cabin
went southwest
w/a .303 and a
half pint of lonesome

at sunset the
wind whistles
the blues through
a ring of bone
blues through
the pine
not stopping
at the tree line
like campfire smoke
you can no longer see
carried by the high wind
through the twisted and broken

looking for kerouac

at night
weekend poets
with walmart berets
search for meaning
in faux jazz joints
haikus are lost
to jazz notes swingin'
from a computer programmed
bose system

brautigan meets bukowski

i had just cut
the hole in the ice
when i got the text
saying you had left
this time for good
it was like the time
when brautigan
met bukowski
in some afternoon bar
and neither
had anything to say
and nobody wrote
a poem about
the other
but drank alone
two stools apart
and here
the lake trout
looks up at me
through wtf eyes
and i say
exactly

bukowski
was always right

bukowski sat
next to
brautigan in
ginos bar
said
hey buddy
you know when
the words go
she'll leave ya
you got
nothing
unless you
buy it
might as well
cash in yr chips

richard looked
at the small pile
of change
beside the
wet coaster
counted forty
five cents
tried to scratch
out a poem
to trade for a beer

nothing

now this is
what i'm talkin
about

bukowski said
rubbing the red
head's thigh up
under her dress

brautigan was
already on the
sidewalk pea coat
collar pulled up
against the north
beach rain
mustache still damp
from the last drops
of beer
45 cents clutched
in his fist
like his last poem
wasn't enough

for anything

written in the key of lonely

brautigan
listened
to hank
williams
the 40
greatest
hits
album
one
by
one
on a
gray
bolinas
day
the
mist
fell
lonesome
and
that
was

enough

a beer with bukowski

sat two stools down
from bukowski
holding up a high-life
he nodded in my direction
downed it
tapped the empty
on the bar

another

i whispered
bartender
tell him i'm a poet

bukowski emptied
another one
tapped it twice
twisted out
his cigarette
went to the john

i leaned in
whatdidhesay

sounding like cagney
& polishing small circles
on the worn bar
he said

who the hell ain't

gone with the wind
for butterfly mcqueen

i met ms mcqueen
in 74
she was onstage in kc
in a starring role
and i cleaned up after
the dinner show
and all the money
went home

she told me once
i would do great things
i told her i wanted to
go into construction
shaking her head
she had the biggest smile
and said that was not
what she saw

she said she didn't care
for streets paved with gold
never believed
in those jesus myths
that her first acting job
was a maid and probably
be her last role as well

that when she did
gone with the wind
she couldn't go to the
premiere
it was whites only

when i said that
was a long time ago
ms mcqueen
she smiled
placed her hand on my
arm and shook her head
no honey
it's not

one last thing

for rosanna

i know we kinda talked about it
but never really nailed it down
so put me in the field where
we watched the sun rise
& and the lunar eclipse
where the goats and donkeys
run wild like kids and colts

put me in the field between
the two oaks so i can
hear the pond frogs at night
where i can see the eagles
in the tree tops and watch the heron
swoop in fishing for dinner
where pearl and thelma would sit
with us under the shade
where the deer would come in
at dusk and eat until dawn

put me in the field so i may
be the first to feel the morning breeze
and hear the song of chuck-wills-widow
and the first whippoorwill of spring

you hear that?

have them bring in a boulder
from our land
to mark the spot
between the two oaks
where i carved your name
deep inside
my heart

Scot Young lives with the woman of his dreams on a ridge top farm in the Missouri Ozarks. He is widely published online and in numerous print anthologies and chapbooks. His first chap *Brautigan Meets Bukowski* is out of print with a copy residing in the Brautiagn Library. He also co-authored with John Dorsey *Head On*. He is the editor of the *Rusty Truck* and *Deuce Coupe*. He and his wife Rosanna are publishers at Rusty Truck Press.